A Trip to the
SCIENCE
MUSEUM
with SESAME STREET

Christy Peterson

Lerner Publications ◆ Minneapolis

Elmo and his friends from *Sesame Street* are going on a field trip, and you're invited! Field trips provide children with the opportunity to explore their communities, visit new places, and experience hands-on learning. This series brings the joys of field trips to your fingertips. Where will you go next?

—Sincerely, the Editors at Sesame Street

TABLE OF CONTENTS

LET'S VISIT A SCIENCE MUSEUM!

Today we're visiting a science museum. We will get to be scientists for the day!

5

Our tour guide says science is all around us. At this museum, we can learn about animals, rocks, outer space, dinosaurs, how things work, and more!

Each exhibit teaches us something new. These bones show us the shape and size of dinosaurs from long ago.

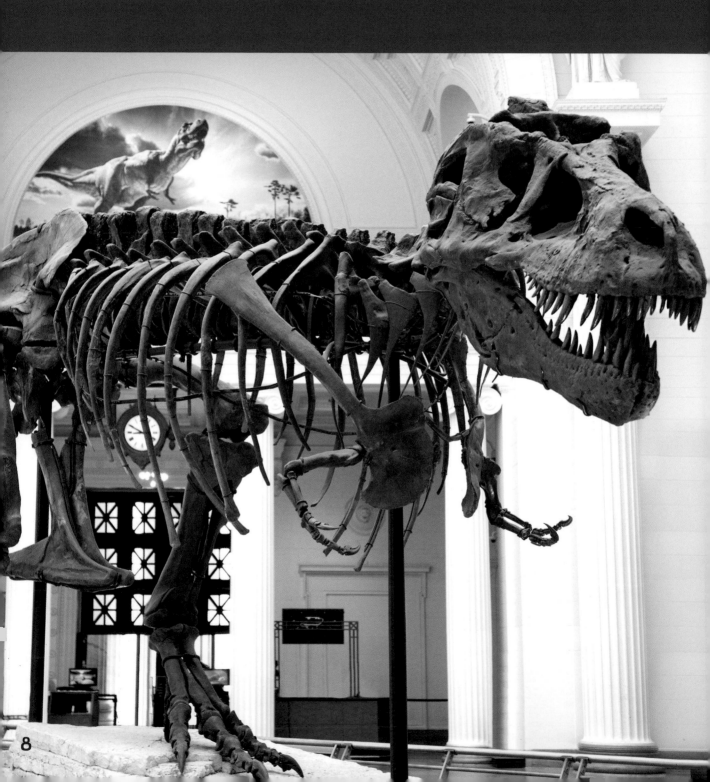

Some exhibits have things to move and touch. At this water table, we learn how some things float and other things sink.

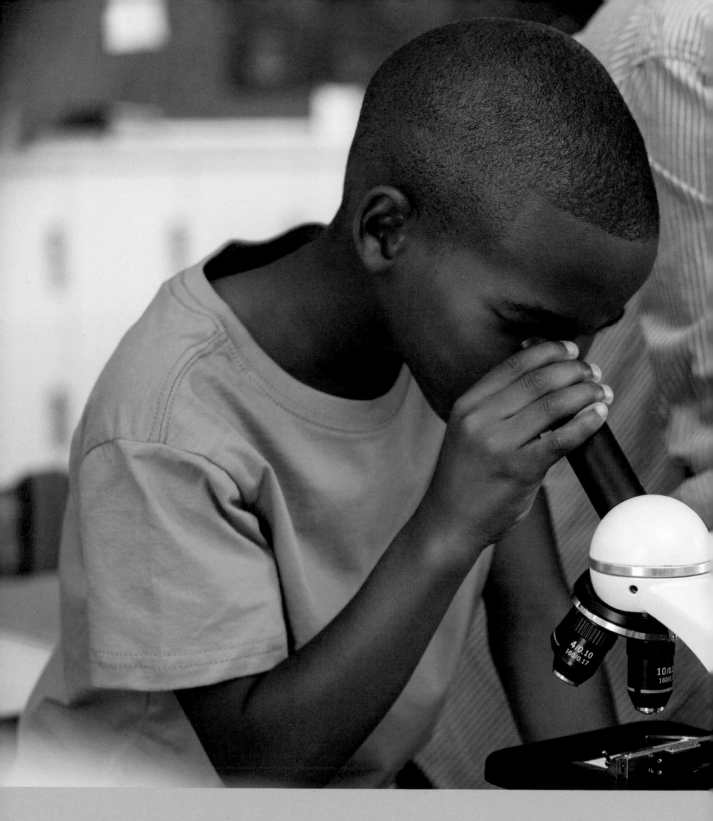

Microscopes help us see very tiny things up close. We look at tiny parts of plants and animals to learn more about them.

Crash! Boom! Bang! The displays in this exhibit help us learn about sound. Sounds can be loud or quiet.

This room is full of rocks! They are all different shapes and colors. Scientists who study rocks are called geologists.

At the end of our trip, we visit the planetarium. It is a big room where we learn about planets and stars.

Science museums help us see science all around us. We can play, explore, and learn about our world there.

I can't wait to visit again!

SCIENCE MUSEUM AT HOME

We can go outside to learn about the world too. Grab a pencil and a notebook. Take a walk in your neighborhood with your grown-up. Draw or write down the things you notice.

- **What is the weather like?**
- **What plants or animals do you see?**
- **What sounds do you hear?**

Share the things you noticed with your friends or family.

GLOSSARY

exhibit: a display in a museum

microscope: a tool that allows you to see tiny objects

museum: a place with objects or displays for visitors to look at

planetarium: a theater where images of stars and planets are projected onto the ceiling

LEARN MORE

Jacoby, Jenny. *Build Your Own Dinosaur Museum*. Oakland: Lonely Planet Kids, 2018.

Peterson, Christy. *A Trip to the Zoo with Sesame Street*. Minneapolis: Lerner Publications, 2022.

Zimmerman, Adeline J. *Museum*. Minneapolis: Jump!, 2021.

INDEX

PHOTO ACKNOWLEDGMENTS

Image credits: Anton_Ivanov/Shutterstock.com, pp. 4–5; FatCamera/E+/Getty Images, p. 6; Monkey Business Images/Shutterstock.com, p. 7; Vlad G/Shutterstock.com, p. 8; DGLimages/Shutterstock.com, p. 10; Rido/Shutterstock.com, pp. 12–13; frantic00/Shutterstock.com, p. 14; Wavebreakmedia/Getty Images, p. 16; Todor Stoyanov/Shutterstock.com, p. 17; Hill Street Studios/DigitalVision/Getty Images, pp. 18–19; Ekpluto/Shutterstock.com, p. 20.

Cover: Monkey Business Images/Shutterstock.com.

Lerner Publications Company
An imprint of Lerner Publishing Group, Inc.
241 First Avenue North
Minneapolis, MN 55401 USA

For reading levels and more information, look up this title at www.lernerbooks.com.

Main body text set in Mikado a.
Typeface provided by HVD Fonts.

Editor: Rebecca Higgins

Library of Congress Cataloging-in-Publication Data

Names: Peterson, Christy, author.
Title: A trip to the science museum with Sesame Street / Christy Peterson.
Description: Minneapolis: Lerner Publications, [2022] | Series: Sesame Street field trips | Includes bibliographic references and index. | Audience: Ages 4–8 | Audience: Grades K–1 | Summary: "Elmo and Sesame Street friends take readers on a tour of a science museum. Readers learn about math, technology, and how to make observations"—Provided by publisher.
Identifiers: LCCN 2021007540 (print) | LCCN 2021007541 (ebook) | ISBN 9781728439150 (library binding) | ISBN 9781728445090 (ebook)
Subjects: LCSH: Science museums—Juvenile literature.
Classification: LCC Q105.A1 P48 2022 (print) | LCC Q105.A1 (ebook) | DDC 507.4—dc23

LC record available at https://lccn.loc.gov/2021007540
LC ebook record available at https://lccn.loc.gov/2021007541

Manufactured in the United States of America
1-49821-49689-8/16/2021